My Life as a Native American

Ann H. Matzke

Educational Media

rourkeeducationalmedia.com

Teacher Notes available at
rem4teachers.com

www.rourkeeducationalmedia.com

PHOTO CREDITS: Cover: © Richard Seeney, subjug, JOE CICAK; Title Page: © Coral Coolahan; Page border: © Jason Lugo; Page 3,10,11,13: © Library of Congress; Page 5: © Linda Steward; Page 6,7: © Helena Lovincic; Page 8: © The Probert Encyclopedia; Page 9: © Andrew Penner; Page 12: © www.gallery.oldbookart.com; Page 14: © Denver Public Library hosted by LOC; Page 15: © John Johnston; Page 16, 21: © Imagesbybarbara; Page 17: © Ralf Hettler; Page 18: © Christopher Hudson; Page 19: © Jon Jordan Spirit of the Eagle Presentations; Page 20: © Bill Perry;

Edited by: Precious McKenzie
Cover design by: Tara Raymo
Interior design by: Renee Brady

Library of Congress PCN Data

My Life as a Native American / Ann H. Matzke
(Little World Social Studies)
ISBN 978-1-61810-141-9(hard cover)(alk. paper)
ISBN 978-1-61810-274-4(soft cover)
Library of Congress Control Number: 2011945868

Rourke Educational Media
Printed in the United States of America,
North Mankato, Minnesota

rourkeeducationalmedia.com
customerservice@rourkeeducationalmedia.com • PO Box 643328 Vero Beach, Florida 32964

I am a Native American. My great grandparents lived on the **Great Plains**. Let me tell you about them.

They lived in family groups, young and old, in one or many communities that formed a **tribe**.

The tribes lived on the Great Plains to follow the buffalo.

Native American Fact

There were many tribes of Native Americans living in North America.

5

My family is Lakota. My great grandparent's home was a **tipi**.

Native American Fact

The covering of a tipi is made from cured buffalo skins that let light in but is waterproof, keeping out wind, rain, ice, and snow.

7

They moved to follow the buffalo, packing their tipi and belongings on a **travois**.

The Arapaho, Blackfoot, Cheyenne, Crow, and Lakota tribes moved about the Great Plains following the buffalo.

The men of my tribe **hunted** buffalo.

Native American Fact

The buffalo provided food, clothing, tools, and shelter. Every part of the buffalo was used, nothing was wasted.

Before the hunt the men in some tribes **performed** the buffalo dance.

Native American Fact

Wearing buffalo masks, the men dance while others sing to attract the buffalo in hope of a great hunt.

Pemmican is one of many dishes made from the buffalo.

Strips of meat are dried in the sunlight.

Wild cherries, sun-dried buffalo meat, and melted fat are pounded together to make a nutritious traveling food, called Pemmican.

Pemmican is a traditional food still eaten today.

Their clothing was made of buckskin, from deer. In the winter they wore heavy robes made from buffalo hides.

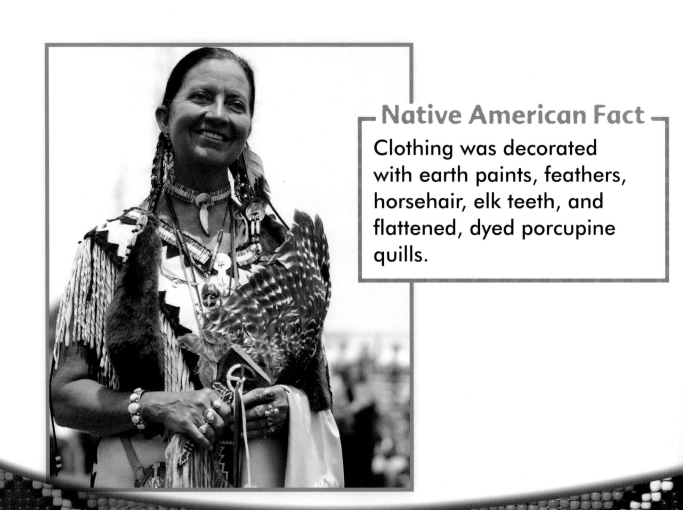

Native American Fact

Clothing was decorated with earth paints, feathers, horsehair, elk teeth, and flattened, dyed porcupine quills.

In the winter they liked to sled.

A thick, heavy buffalo hide kept people warm while sledding.

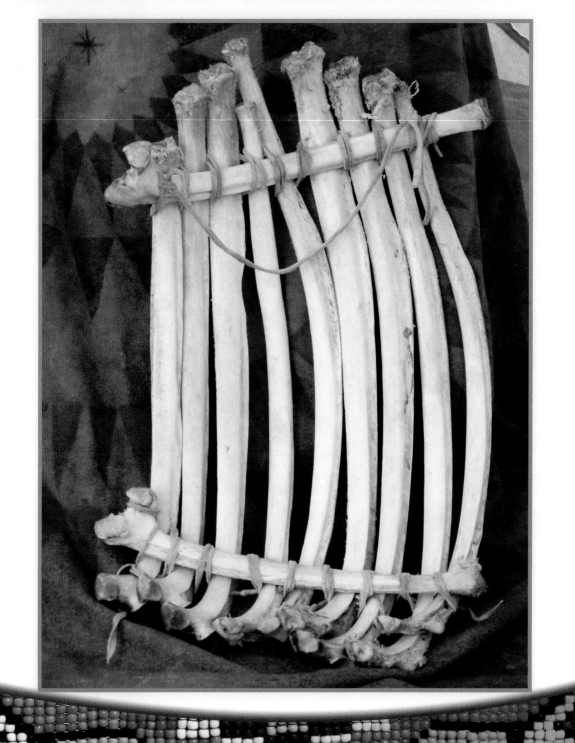

We are a proud people, carrying on the traditions of our great grandparents.

Drums, dance, and native clothing are part of our culture.

Picture Glossary

Great Plains (grayt planes): Grassland prairies covering a large section in the middle of the United States.

hunted (HUHNT-id): To chase on foot or horse and then to kill wild animals for food.

performed (pur-FORMD): To give a show in public.

 **tipi** (TEE-pee): Lakota name for a cone shaped home made from buffalo skins stitched together and stretched around many long poles.

 **travois** (tra-VOICE): Two tipi poles lashed together with a strip of rawhide form a V-shaped frame pulled by a horse or dog for moving belongings.

 **tribe** (tribe): People living together who share the same background, customs, language, and laws.

Index

Websites

www.americanhistory.si.edu/kids/buffalo/index.html

nativeamericans.mrdonn.org/plains.html

www.native-languages.org/kids.htm

About the Author

Ann H. Matzke is a children's librarian. She has an MFA in Writing for children and young adults from Hamline University. Ann lives on the Great Plains in Gothenburg, Nebraska, where the Lakota and other native tribes once followed the buffalo.

Ask The Author!
www.rem4students.com